Poem 2016

A Treasure Trove Of Fun

Edited By Jenni Bannister

First published in Great Britain in 2016 by:

Coltsfoot Drive
Peterborough
PE2 9BF
Telephone: 01733 890066
Website: www.youngwriters.co.uk

Foreword

Young Writers was established in 1991 with the aim of encouraging writing skills in young people and giving them the opportunity to see their work in print. Poetry is a wonderful way to introduce young children to the idea of rhyme and rhythm and helps learning and development of communication, language and literacy skills.

'My First Poem' was created to introduce nursery and preschool children to this wonderful world of poetry. They were given a template to fill in with their own words, creating a poem that was all about them.

We are proud to present the resulting collection of personal and touching poems in this anthology, which can be treasured for years to come.

Jenni Bannister
Editorial Manager

Contents

Hayden Graham (4) 38
Elsie Linforth (4) 39
Sam Connor (3) 40
Remany Grace Ullyott (4) 41
Travis Brackenbury (4) 42

Children's Choice Nursery, Whitley Bay

Isaac Stirland (4) 43
Maya Jones (3) 44
Isabella Bush-Clark (4) 45
George Crackett (4) 46

Clever Cloggs Day Nursery, Dunmow

Kieran Robin Andrew 47
Bearman (4)
Faith Baydemir (4) 48
Kirsty Anne Munro (4) 49
Bella Hammond (4) 50
Grace Hudgell (3) 51

Cogenhoe Preschool, Northampton

James John Mackay (4) 52
Leighton Hearn Reeves (3) 53
John Junior Bennett (4) 54
Michael Godfrey (4) 55
Willow Baker-Jones (2) 56
Taya Young (3) 57
Roan Garratt (3) 58

Foulsham & Bintree Playgroup, Dereham

Ruben John Royston (3) 59
Harley Wiseman-Marshall (3) 60
Finley Rourke (3) 61
Bethany Leeder (2) 62

Emilia Allen (2) 63
Harvey Patrick (2) 64
Leah Paige Westlake (3) 65
Ellie Chinn (3) 66

Giggles Of Lytham, Lytham St Annes

Tia Porter (4) 67
Sophia Alexa Taylor (4) 68
Meher Diwaker (4) 69
Ruby Olivia Hibbert (3) 70
Emily Southworth (4) 71
Riley James Nicholson (4) 72
Pixie Margaret Leaver (4) 73
Ben Flood (4) 74
Leo White (4) 75

Happy Jacks Day Nursery, Littleborough

Riley Downes (3) 76
Louis John Philip Braund (3) 77
Leo Giddins 78
Khaleesi Sharon Lorna 79
Carroll (3)
Ruby Marie Gooding (2) 80
Isabelle Bostock (3) 81
Skye Ellouise Parsons (3) 82
Kristoff White Ogu (2) 83
Miles Parfitt (2) 84
Brandon Lee Brooks (3) 85
Grayson Howard (3) 86

Happylands Private Day Nursery, Wardon

Isabelle Sparkes (4) 87

Humshaugh & District Preschool, Hexham

Tobias Schatzberger (3)	88
Callum Wood (4)	89
Teddy James McKenzie (3)	90
Mia Robinson (3)	91

Little Oaks Day Nursery, Newcastle

Winston Richards (3)	92
Sebastian Harris (3)	93
Everleigh Tomlinson (3)	94
Jan Choina (3)	95
Hope Elizabeth Evans (3)	96
Alexander Wyrwa (3)	97
Samar Singh Zandu (3)	98
Riley Barnett (3)	99
Maxi Clews (4)	100
Heidi Sharp (3)	101
Amber Badu (3)	102

Little Scallywags Ltd, Crieff

Davi Esteves (3)	103
Lachlan Stewart (3)	104
Dylan Rennie (3)	105

Metheringham Preschool, Lincoln

Elizabeth Mary Pearse (4)	106
Ella May Reed (4)	107

Muddy Boots Preschool, Northampton

Harley Kye Redden (3)	108
Ellis Middleton-Hale (3)	109
Kobie Loveridge (3)	110
Toby Evans (4)	111
Jack Cobain Davies (4)	112

Ollie Clarke (4)	113
Evie Miller (3)	114
Lily Rose Quigley (4)	115
Molly Tillett (4)	116
Lily Downer (3)	117
Emmeline Violet Moore (4)	118
Marlie Florence Chelsey Ellaby (3)	119
Jenson Budd (4)	120
Harry Sweeney (2)	121
Leila Leonard (4)	122
Lucy Burchell (3)	123
Jack Hudson-Pridmore (3)	124
Teagan Linnell (2)	125
Dylan Feasey (4)	126
Blake Peter Noel Boulter (3)	127
Ted Murray (3)	128
Tommy Jeffery (4)	129
Oscar Benedetti (3)	130
Bowan Thomas-Wainwright (3)	131
Mackenzie Katie Thomas-Wainwright (4)	132

Napley Lodge Farm Day Nursery, Market Drayton

Alfie Ebrey (3)	133

Peter Pan Preschool, Nuneaton

Bonnie Sadie Withers (3)	134
Evie McHugh (3)	135
Kaytlin Elizabeth Bradford (4)	136
Charlie Joe Briggs (3)	137
Britanny Faith Bongayen Che (3)	138
Teddy Saul Twamley (3)	139
Tulisa Ann Phythian (3)	140
Tiara Rai (4)	141
Jack Cairns (4)	142

Ravensmere Arc, Beccles

Seashells Nursery, Mablethorpe

Serendipitys Day Nursery, Newark

Shardlow Hall Private Day Nursery, Derby

Sinfin Community Childcare, Derby

St Michael's Preschool, Peterborough

Stepping Stones Preschool, Smethwick

Sunny Days Preschool, High Wycombe

Teddies Day Nursery, Oldham

Sabrina Amara Hussain (4)	190
Jaymee Ann Corbishley (4)	191
Chiasa Etugo (4)	192
Holly Mari-Beth Walsh (4)	193
Brayden Ashworth (3)	194
Nevaeh Caines-Rahman (4)	195
George Roy Grady (4)	196
Orla Mary Corbishley (4)	197

The Poems

My First Poem

My name is Uma and I go to preschool,

My best friend is Aiofe, who is really cool.

I watch cartoons on TV,

Playing in my teepee is lots of fun for me.

I just love ham sandwiches to eat,

And sometimes marshmallows for a treat.

Pink is a colour I like a lot,

My unicorn is the best present I ever got.

My favourite person is Mummy who is a gem,

So this, my first poem, is just for them!

Uma Patel (3)

My First Poem

My name is **Lewis** and I go to preschool,

My best friend is **Frankie**, who is really cool.

I watch **Team Umizoomi** on TV,

Playing **catch** is lots of fun for me.

I just love **cheesy pasta** to eat,

And sometimes **biscuits** for a treat.

Blue is a colour I like a lot,

My **Track Master Thomas** is the best present I

ever got.

My favourite person is **Daddy**, who is a gem,

So this, my first poem, is just for them!

Lewis James Bishop (4)

My First Poem

My name is Ivy and I go to preschool,

My best friends are Ariella and Ryan, who are

really cool.

I watch Frozen on TV,

Playing My Littlest Pet Shop is lots of fun for me.

I just love yoghurt to eat,

And sometimes chocolate for a treat.

Purple and red are colours I like a lot,

My Anna and Elsa are the best presents I ever got.

My favourite person is Julia, who is a gem,

So this, my first poem, is just for them!

Ivy Rose Stokes (4)

All My Friends Childcare Ltd, Gloucester

My First Poem

My name is Ramyah and I go to preschool,
My best friend is Darpad, who is really cool.
I watch Peppa Pig on TV,
Playing dolls is lots of fun for me.
I just love chicken, rice and gravy to eat,
And sometimes sweets for a treat.
Blue is a colour I like a lot,
My nail polish is the best present I ever got.
My favourite person is Bronte, who is a gem,
So this, my first poem, is just for them!

Ramyah Nairn (4)

All My Friends Childcare Ltd, Gloucester

My First Poem

My name is **Elliot** and I go to preschool,

My best friends are **Elijah, Mummy and Daddy**,

who are really cool.

I watch **Zombies** on TV,

Playing **with Lego** is lots of fun for me.

I just love **pancakes** to eat,

And sometimes **a doughnut** for a treat.

Purple is a colour I like a lot,

My **motorbike** is the best present I ever got.

My favourite person is **Mummy**, who is a gem,

So this, my first poem, is just for them!

Elliot Peter Andrew Woodgate (4)

All My Friends Childcare Ltd, Gloucester

My First Poem

My name is Lucy and I go to preschool,

My best friend is Mummy, who is really cool.

I watch PAW Patrol on TV,

Playing with the babies is lots of fun for me.

I just love chicken to eat,

And sometimes fruit for a treat.

Pink is a colour I like a lot,

My cat is the best present I ever got.

My favourite person is Emily, who is a gem,

So this, my first poem, is just for them!

Lucy Luton (3)

All My Friends Childcare Ltd, Gloucester

My First Poem

My name is Phoebe and I go to preschool,

My best friend is Isla, who is really cool.

I watch CBeebies on TV,

Playing football is lots of fun for me.

I just love strawberries to eat,

And sometimes sweets and chocolate for a treat.

Yellow is a colour I like a lot,

My horse and yo-yo are the best presents I ever got.

My favourite people are Mummy and Daddy, who are gems,

So this, my first poem, is just for them!

Phoebe Alexander (3)

All My Friends Childcare Ltd, Gloucester

7

My First Poem

My name is Jack and I go to preschool,

My best friend is Finley Marsh, who is really cool.

I watch Blaze and the Monster Machines on TV,

Playing marbles and cars is lots of fun for me.

I just love omelettes to eat,

And sometimes chocolate for a treat.

Blue is a colour I like a lot,

My chickens are the best present I ever got.

My favourite person is my daddy, who is a gem,

So this, my first poem, is just for them!

Jack James Kettle (3)

Banana Moon Baddesley Ensor Day Nursery, Nr Atherstone

My First Poem

My name is Sophie and I go to preschool,

My best friend is Noah, who is really cool.

I watch Peppa Pig on TV,

Playing ring-a-ring o' roses is lots of fun for me.

I just love beef to eat,

And sometimes chocolate for a treat.

Purple is a colour I like a lot,

My Sylvanian cottage is the best present I ever got.

My favourite person is Grandpa, who is a gem,

So this, my first poem, is just for them!

Sophie Ross (3)

Banana Moon Baddesley Ensor Day Nursery, Nr Atherstone

My First Poem

My name is Finley and I go to preschool,

My best friend is Harry, who is really cool.

I watch Peter Rabbit on TV,

Playing Snakes and Ladders is lots of fun for me.

I just love chocolate and bananas to eat,

And sometimes squidgy yoghurt and crisps for

a treat.

Red is a colour I like a lot,

My castle is the best present I ever got.

My favourite people are Gran and Nanny, who

are gems,

So this, my first poem, is just for them!

Finley Gayton (3)

Banana Moon Baddesley Ensor Day Nursery, Nr Atherstone

My First Poem

My name is Aurelia and I go to preschool,
My best friend is Mischa, who is really cool.
I watch Frozen Elsa on TV,
Playing cats is lots of fun for me.
I just love carrots to eat,
And sometimes chocolate for a treat.
Yellow is a colour I like a lot,
My dinosaur is the best present I ever got.
My favourite person is Mischa, who is a gem,
So this, my first poem, is just for them!

Aurelia Mania (4)

Barhill Preschool Playgroup, Cambridge

My First Poem

My name is **Tom** and I go to preschool,

My best friend is **Nora**, who is really cool.

I watch **Bob the Builder** on TV,

Playing **animals** is lots of fun for me.

I just love **pasta** to eat,

And sometimes **ice cream** for a treat.

White is a colour I like a lot,

My **book** is the best present I ever got.

My favourite person is **Mummy**, who is a gem,

So this, my first poem, is just for them!

Tom McArthur (3)
Barhill Preschool Playgroup, Cambridge

My First Poem

My name is **Tara** and I go to preschool,

My best friends are **Nora and Flynn**, who are

really cool.

I watch **Blaze** on TV,

Playing **with my Frozen dolls** is lots of fun for me.

I just love **bananas** to eat,

And sometimes **waffles** for a treat.

Purple is a colour I like a lot,

My **Elsa dolls** are the best presents I ever got.

My favourite person is **Mummy**, who is a gem,

So this, my first poem, is just for them!

Tara Lee (3)

Barhill Preschool Playgroup, Cambridge

My First Poem

My name is Seweryn and I go to preschool,

My best friend is Gaby, who is really cool.

I watch Surprise Eggs on YouTube,

Playing with buses is lots of fun for me.

I just love crisps to eat,

And sometimes chocolate for a treat.

Green is a colour I like a lot,

My puzzle is the best present I ever got.

My favourite person is Mummy, who is a gem,

So this, my first poem, is just for them!

Seweryn Kielczewski (3)

Barhill Preschool Playgroup, Cambridge

My First Poem

My name is Rafaella and I go to preschool,

My best friends are Lech and Nicolas, who are

really cool.

I watch Frozen on TV,

Playing with my cuddly dog, Sky, is lots of fun

for me.

I just love apples to eat,

And sometimes cake for a treat.

Pink is a colour I like a lot,

My Elsa dress is the best present I ever got.

My favourite people are Mummy and Daddy, who

are gems,

So this, my first poem, is just for them!

Rafaella Warecha (4)
Barhill Preschool Playgroup, Cambridge

My First Poem

My name is Flynn and I go to preschool,

My best friend is Nora, who is really cool.

I watch Peppa Pig and Minions on TV,

Playing with trains is lots of fun for me.

I just love rice to eat,

And sometimes ice cream for a treat.

Blue is a colour I like a lot,

My Bumblebee is the best present I ever got.

My favourite person is Mummy, who is a gem,

So this, my first poem, is just for them!

Flynn Hanquez (3)
Barhill Preschool Playgroup, Cambridge

My First Poem

My name is Summer and I go to preschool,
My best friend is Lotti, who is really cool.
I watch Peppa Pig and Cinderella on TV,
Playing doctors and Peppa Pig is lots of fun for me.
I just love fish fingers to eat,
And sometimes sweeties for a treat.
Red and purple are colours I like a lot,
My unicorn is the best present I ever got.
My favourite person is Lotti, who is a gem,
So this, my first poem, is just for them!

Summer Harris (3)
Beckley Preschool, Beckley

My First Poem

My name is Arthur and I go to preschool,

My best friend is Joey, who is really cool.

I watch CBeebies on TV,

Playing with tractors is lots of fun for me.

I just love Marmite on toast to eat,

And sometimes doughnuts for a treat.

Blue is a colour I like a lot,

My combine harvester is the best present I ever got.

My favourite person is my mummy, who is a gem,

So this, my first poem, is just for them!

Arthur Dobson (4)

Beckley Preschool, Beckley

My First Poem

My name is Darcie and I go to preschool,
My best friend is Arthur, who is really cool.
I watch Peppa Pig on TV,
Playing Playmobil is lots of fun for me.
I just love ham sandwiches to eat,
And sometimes pizza for a treat.
Pink is a colour I like a lot,
My Barbie doctor is the best present I ever got.
My favourite person is Mummy, who is a gem,
So this, my first poem, is just for them!

Darcie Ongley (3)
Beckley Preschool, Beckley

My First Poem

My name is Joey and I go to preschool,

My best friend is Jack, who is really cool.

I watch Bing on TV,

Playing with Arthur is lots of fun for me.

I just love Coco Pops to eat,

And sometimes chocolate coins for a treat.

Red is a colour I like a lot,

My iPad is the best present I ever got.

My favourite person is Mikey, who is a gem,

So this, my first poem, is just for them!

Joey Alexander-Crossan (3)

Beckley Preschool, Beckley

My First Poem

My name is Gracie and I go to preschool,

My best friends are Daphne, Felicity and Fern,

who are really cool.

I watch Frozen on TV,

Playing with Jackie is lots of fun for me.

I just love carrots to eat,

And sometimes chocolate for a treat.

Blue and pink are colours I like a lot,

My pink pram is the best present I ever got.

My favourite person is Mummy, who is a gem,

So this, my first poem, is just for them!

Gracie Knight (4)

Beckley Preschool, Beckley

My First Poem

My name is Ronnie and I go to preschool,

My best friends are Indie and Felicity, who are

really cool.

I watch Spider-Man, Peppa Pig and Ben

& Holly on TV,

Playing with cars and fixing is lots of fun for me.

I just love crackers, cheese and apples to eat,

And sometimes chocolate for a treat.

Brown is a colour I like a lot,

My bike is the best present I ever got.

My favourite people are Nana and Grandad, who

are gems,

So this, my first poem, is just for them!

Ronnie Knight (4)

Beckley Preschool, Beckley

My First Poem

My name is **Abigail** and I go to preschool,

My best friend is **Jacob**, who is really cool.

I watch **King Julien** on TV,

Playing **with Jacob** is lots of fun for me.

I just love **pizza** to eat,

And sometimes **chocolate or oranges** for a treat.

Pink is a colour I like a lot,

My **Elsa with a microphone** is the best present I ever got.

My favourite person is **Bethany**, who is a gem,

So this, my first poem, is just for them!

Abigail Sherlock (3)

Bluebell Lodge Nursery, Blackpool

My First Poem

My name is Erin and I go to preschool,

My best friends are Jack and Aimee, who are

really cool.

I watch Little Princess and PAW Patrol on TV,

Playing with dollies is lots of fun for me.

I just love fruit flan to eat,

And sometimes chocolate for a treat.

Pink is a colour I like a lot,

My bike is the best present I ever got.

My favourite person is Mummy, who is a gem,

So this, my first poem, is just for them!

Erin Poppy-Mae Boardman (4)

Bluebell Lodge Nursery, Blackpool

My First Poem

My name is Samuel and I go to preschool,
My best friend is Cody, who is really cool.
I watch Peppa Pig on TV,
Playing with toys is lots of fun for me.
I just love fish fingers to eat,
And sometimes sweeties for a treat.
Blue is a colour I like a lot,
My Mousetrap is the best present I ever got.
My favourite person is Mummy, who is a gem,
So this, my first poem, is just for them!

Samuel Wallace (4)
Bluebell Lodge Nursery, Blackpool

My First Poem

My name is Mia and I go to preschool,

My best friends are Millie and Freya, who are

really cool.

I watch Minions on TV,

Playing sharks is lots of fun for me.

I just love pizza and yoghurt to eat,

And sometimes penguin sweeties for a treat.

Pink is a colour I like a lot,

My big talking, walking dinosaur is the best

present I ever got.

My favourite people are Mummy, Daddy and

Harry, who are gems,

So this, my first poem, is just for them!

Mia Louise Ruth Shelliker (4)

Bluebell Lodge Nursery, Blackpool

My First Poem

My name is Freya and I go to preschool,
My best friend is Cody, who is really cool.
I watch CBeebies on TV,
Playing dancing is lots of fun for me.
I just love pasta to eat,
And sometimes ice cream for a treat.
Pink is a colour I like a lot,
My tab is the best present I ever got.
My favourite person is Mummy, who is a gem,
So this, my first poem, is just for them!

Freya Erskine (4)
Bluebell Lodge Nursery, Blackpool

My First Poem

My name is Lily and I go to preschool,

My best friends are Jacob and Jack, who are

really cool.

I watch Superman on TV,

Playing football is lots of fun for me.

I just love sausage and beans to eat,

And sometimes choc choc for a treat.

Black is a colour I like a lot,

My Rose Petal cottage is the best present I

ever got.

My favourite person is Mummy, who is a gem,

So this, my first poem, is just for them!

Lily Summer Peel (3)

Bluebell Lodge Nursery, Blackpool

My First Poem

My name is Mia and I go to preschool,

My best friend is Freya, who is really cool.

I watch Alvin on TV,

Playing Frozen is lots of fun for me.

I just love fish pie to eat,

And sometimes a Kinder egg for a treat.

Purple is a colour I like a lot,

My iPad is the best present I ever got.

My favourite person is Grandad, who is a gem,

So this, my first poem, is just for them!

Mia Breakell (4)

Bluebell Lodge Nursery, Blackpool

29

My First Poem

My name is Eva and I go to preschool,

My best friend is Mummy, who is really cool.

I watch Kung Fu Panda on TV,

Playing with my doll's house is lots of fun for me.

I just love ham to eat,

And sometimes chocolate for a treat.

Blue is a colour I like a lot,

My bear is the best present I ever got.

My favourite person is Mummy, who is a gem,

So this, my first poem, is just for them!

Eva Connie Phillips (3)
Butterflies Day Nursery, Leeds

My First Poem

My name is Riley and I go to preschool,

My best friend is Lily, who is really cool.

I watch Peppa Pig on TV,

Playing Teenage Mutant Ninja Turtles is lots of

fun for me.

I just love sausages to eat,

And sometimes chocolate for a treat.

Green is a colour I like a lot,

My Donatello light is the best present I ever got.

My favourite person is Tallulah, who is a gem,

So this, my first poem, is just for them!

Riley Adam Cater (3)

Butterflies Day Nursery, Leeds

My First Poem

My name is Max and I go to preschool,
My best friend is Isaac, who is really cool.
I watch PAW Patrol on TV,
Playing with cars is lots of fun for me.
I just love sausages to eat,
And sometimes ice cream for a treat.
Blue is a colour I like a lot,
My ball is the best present I ever got.
My favourite person is Daddy, who is a gem,
So this, my first poem, is just for them!

Max Szugalski (3)
Butterflies Day Nursery, Leeds

My First Poem

My name is Alannah and I go to preschool,

My best friend is my mummy, who is really cool.

I watch Peppa Pig on TV,

Playing with my dollies is lots of fun for me.

I just love chicken nuggets to eat,

And sometimes crisps for a treat.

Red is a colour I like a lot,

My Snow White dress is the best present I ever got.

My favourite person is Snow White, who is a gem,

So this, my first poem, is just for them!

Alannah Haigh (3)
Butterflies Day Nursery, Leeds

My First Poem

My name is Lilly and I go to preschool,

My best friend is Darcy, who is really cool.

I watch Peppa Pig on TV,

Playing with my teddy bear is lots of fun for me.

I just love spaghetti to eat,

And sometimes yoghurt for a treat.

Purple is a colour I like a lot,

My Olaf pyjamas are the best present I ever got.

My favourite person is Mummy, who is a gem,

So this, my first poem, is just for them!

Lilly Mortimer (3)

Butterflies Day Nursery, Leeds

My First Poem

My name is Bobby and I go to preschool,

My best friend is Isabelle, who is really cool.

I watch Peppa Pig on TV,

Playing on my motorbike is lots of fun for me.

I just love McDonald's to eat,

And sometimes ice cream for a treat.

Black is a colour I like a lot,

My motorbike is the best present I ever got.

My favourite people are Mummy and Daddy, who

are gems,

So this, my first poem, is just for them!

Bobby Taylor (3)
Butterflies Day Nursery, Leeds

My First Poem

My name is Charlize and I go to preschool,

My best friend is Jessica, who is really cool.

I watch dinosaurs on TV,

Playing monkey is lots of fun for me.

I just love pasta to eat,

And sometimes sweets for a treat.

Yellow is a colour I like a lot,

My bike is the best present I ever got.

My favourite person is Daddy, who is a gem,

So this, my first poem, is just for them!

Charlize Townsend (3)

Caythorpe Preschool, Grantham

My First Poem

My name is Ayla and I go to preschool,
My best friend is Remony, who is really cool.
I watch Mr Tumble on TV,
Playing teddy bears is lots of fun for me.
I just love vegetables to eat,
And sometimes chocolate for a treat.
Blue is a colour I like a lot,
My bike is the best present I ever got.
My favourite person is Mama, who is a gem,
So this, my first poem, is just for them!

Ayla Staff (3)
Caythorpe Preschool, Grantham

My First Poem

My name is **Hayden** and I go to preschool,

My best friend is **Benji**, who is really cool.

I watch **Strawberry Shortcake** on TV,

Playing **with figures** is lots of fun for me.

I just love **sandwiches** to eat,

And sometimes **minty chocolate biscuits** for

a treat.

Green is a colour I like a lot,

My **PAW Patrol Lorry** is the best present I ever got.

My favourite person is **Daddy**, who is a gem,

So this, my first poem, is just for them!

Hayden Graham (4)

Caythorpe Preschool, Grantham

My First Poem

My name is Elsie and I go to preschool,

My best friend is Marie, who is really cool.

I watch Mr Tumble on TV,

Playing jigsaws is lots of fun for me.

I just love sausages to eat,

And sometimes chocolate for a treat.

Pink is a colour I like a lot,

My book is the best present I ever got.

My favourite person is Granny Joan, who is a gem,

So this, my first poem, is just for them!

Elsie Linforth (4)

Caythorpe Preschool, Grantham

My First Poem

My name is Sam and I go to preschool,

My best friend is Charlotte, who is really cool.

I watch Bubble Guppies on TV,

Playing spaceships is lots of fun for me.

I just love vegetables to eat,

And sometimes biscuits for a treat.

Blue is a colour I like a lot,

My dinosaur is the best present I ever got.

My favourite person is Mummy, who is a gem,

So this, my first poem, is just for them!

Sam Connor (3)

Caythorpe Preschool, Grantham

My First Poem

My name is Remany and I go to preschool,

My best friend is Maja, who is really cool.

I watch Frozen on TV,

Playing puzzles is lots of fun for me.

I just love croissants to eat,

And sometimes sweets for a treat.

Purple is a colour I like a lot,

My make-up is the best present I ever got.

My favourite person is Daddy, who is a gem,

So this, my first poem, is just for them!

Remany Grace Ullyott (4)

Caythorpe Preschool, Grantham

41

My First Poem

My name is **Travis** and I go to preschool,

My best friend is **Leon**, who is really cool.

I watch **PAW Patrol** on TV,

Playing **castles** is lots of fun for me.

I just love **crisps** to eat,

And sometimes **sweets** for a treat.

White is a colour I like a lot,

My **bike** is the best present I ever got.

My favourite person is **Dad**, who is a gem,

So this, my first poem, is just for them!

Travis Brackenbury (4)

Caythorpe Preschool, Grantham

My First Poem

My name is Isaac and I go to preschool,

My best friend is Louie, who is really cool.

I watch trains on TV,

Playing with diggers is lots of fun for me.

I just love chocolate to eat,

And sometimes sweeties for a treat.

Red is a colour I like a lot,

My numbers are the best present I ever got.

My favourite person is Mummy, who is a gem,

So this, my first poem, is just for them!

Isaac Stirland (4)

Children's Choice Nursery, Whitley Bay

My First Poem

My name is Maya and I go to preschool,

My best friend is Lottie, who is really cool.

I watch Mr Tumble on TV,

Playing dinosaurs is lots of fun for me.

I just love Rice Krispies to eat,

And sometimes fruit for a treat.

Pink is a colour I like a lot,

My doll is the best present I ever got.

My favourite person is Grandma, who is a gem,

So this, my first poem, is just for them!

Maya Jones (3)
Children's Choice Nursery, Whitley Bay

My First Poem

My name is Isabella and I go to preschool,

My best friend is George, who is really cool.

I watch Busy Town on TV,

Playing puppy dog nursery is lots of fun for me.

I just love cheesy pasta to eat,

And sometimes chocolate for a treat.

Pink is a colour I like a lot,

My Easter bunny is the best present I ever got.

My favourite person is Mummy, who is a gem,

So this, my first poem, is just for them!

Isabella Bush-Clark (4)

Children's Choice Nursery, Whitley Bay

My First Poem

My name is George and I go to preschool,

My best friend is Joseph, who is really cool.

I watch Tarzan on TV,

Playing with trains is lots of fun for me.

I just love sausages to eat,

And sometimes sweets for a treat.

Orange is a colour I like a lot,

My bike is the best present I ever got.

My favourite person is Isabelle, who is a gem,

So this, my first poem, is just for them!

George Crackett (4)
Children's Choice Nursery, Whitley Bay

My First Poem

My name is **Kieran** and I go to preschool,

My best friend is **Kirsty**, who is really cool.

I watch **Little Mix** on TV,

Playing **with Lego** is lots of fun for me.

I just love **fish fingers** to eat,

And sometimes **sweets** for a treat.

Red is a colour I like a lot,

My **Power Ranger** is the best present I ever got.

My favourite people are **Mummy and Daddy**, who are gems,

So this, my first poem, is just for them!

Kieran Robin Andrew Bearman (4)

Clever Cloggs Day Nursery, Dunmow

My First Poem

My name is **Faith** and I go to preschool,

My best friend is **Maisie**, who is really cool.

I watch **Thomas** on TV,

Playing **with friends** is lots of fun for me.

I just love **apples** to eat,

And sometimes **sweets** for a treat.

Pink is a colour I like a lot,

My **bracelet** is the best present I ever got.

My favourite person is **Mummy**, who is a gem,

So this, my first poem, is just for them!

Faith Baydemir (4)

Clever Cloggs Day Nursery, Dunmow

My First Poem

My name is **Kirsty** and I go to preschool,
My best friend is **Faith**, who is really cool.
I watch **Frozen** on TV,
Playing **dress up** is lots of fun for me.
I just love **pasta** to eat,
And sometimes **chocolate** for a treat.
Purple is a colour I like a lot,
My **doll** is the best present I ever got.
My favourite person is **Mummy**, who is a gem,
So this, my first poem, is just for them!

Kirsty Anne Munro (4)
Clever Cloggs Day Nursery, Dunmow

My First Poem

My name is **Bella** and I go to preschool,

My best friend is **Kirsty**, who is really cool.

I watch **Frozen** on TV,

Playing **and dressing up** are lots of fun for me.

I just love **oranges** to eat,

And sometimes **chocolate** for a treat.

Pink is a colour I like a lot,

My **Elsa doll** is the best present I ever got.

My favourite person is **Mummy**, who is a gem,

So this, my first poem, is just for them!

Bella Hammond (4)

Clever Cloggs Day Nursery, Dunmow

My First Poem

My name is **Grace** and I go to preschool,

My best friend is **Isabella**, who is really cool.

I watch **Blaze** on TV,

Playing **with cats and tag** are lots of fun for me.

I just love **carrots** to eat,

And sometimes **sweets** for a treat.

Pink is a colour I like a lot,

My **talking baby** is the best present I ever got.

My favourite people are **Mummy and Nana**, who are gems,

So this, my first poem, is just for them!

Grace Hudgell (3)

Clever Cloggs Day Nursery, Dunmow

My First Poem

My name is JJ and I go to preschool,

My best friend is Coco, who is really cool.

I watch Rudolph the Red Nose Reindeer on TV,

Playing with Play-Doh is lots of fun for me.

I just love carrots to eat,

And sometimes Easter eggs for a treat.

Blue and green are colours I like a lot,

My car is the best present I ever got.

My favourite person is Layla, who is a gem,

So this, my first poem, is just for them!

James John Mackay (4)

Cogenhoe Preschool, Northampton

My First Poem

My name is Leighton and I go to preschool,

My best friend is Eliza, who is really cool.

I watch CBeebies on TV,

Playing with Peppa Pig is lots of fun for me.

I just love plain chicken to eat,

And sometimes porridge for a treat.

Yellow is a colour I like a lot,

My control car is the best present I ever got.

My favourite person is Mummy, who is a gem,

So this, my first poem, is just for them!

Leighton Hearn Reeves (3)

Cogenhoe Preschool, Northampton

My First Poem

My name is John and I go to preschool,

My best friend is Coco, who is really cool.

I watch Woody and Buzz on TV,

Playing Buzz and Woody is lots of fun for me.

I just love sweetcorn, rice and pasta to eat,

And sometimes a chocolate bar for a treat.

Blue is a colour I like a lot,

My dinosaurs are the best presents I ever got.

My favourite people are Mummy, Daddy and Coco,

who are gems,

So this, my first poem, is just for them!

John Junior Bennett (4)

Cogenhoe Preschool, Northampton

My First Poem

My name is Michael and I go to preschool,

My best friend is Ellie, who is really cool.

I watch Peter Rabbit on TV,

Playing outside is lots of fun for me.

I just love yoghurt, bacon and ham to eat,

And sometimes birthday cake with lots of
yummy things on top for a treat.

Yellow and blue are colours I like a lot,

My real camera is the best present I ever got.

My favourite people are Mummy, Anna
and Claudia, who are gems,

So this, my first poem, is just for them!

Michael Godfrey (4)

Cogenhoe Preschool, Northampton

My First Poem

My name is Willow and I go to preschool,

My best friend is my baby, Georgie, who is really cool.

I watch Doc McStuffins on TV,

Playing with Holly is lots of fun for me.

I just love jam and chocolate toast to eat,

And sometimes sweeties for a treat.

Purple is a colour I like a lot,

My doll is the best present I ever got.

My favourite person is Mummy, who is a gem,

So this, my first poem, is just for them!

Willow Baker-Jones (2)

Cogenhoe Preschool, Northampton

My First Poem

My name is Taya and I go to preschool,

My best friend is Eliza, who is really cool.

I watch PAW Patrol on TV,

Playing with Olaf is lots of fun for me.

I just love chicken and pork to eat,

And sometimes an Easter egg for a treat.

Pink is a colour I like a lot,

My Pop-Up Pirate is the best present I ever got.

My favourite people are Nanny, Daddy
and Mummy, who are gems,

So this, my first poem, is just for them!

Taya Young (3)

Cogenhoe Preschool, Northampton

My First Poem

My name is Roan and I go to preschool,

My best friend is George, who is really cool.

I watch Cars on TV,

Playing Lightning McQueen is lots of fun for me.

I just love brioche to eat,

And sometimes cake for a treat.

Red is a colour I like a lot,

My books are the best presents I ever got.

My favourite person is Daddy, who is a gem,

So this, my first poem, is just for them!

Roan Garratt (3)

Cogenhoe Preschool, Northampton

My First Poem

My name is Ruben and I go to preschool,

My best friend is Broden, who is really cool.

I watch PAW Patrol on TV,

Playing catch the fish and Scalextric are lots of fun for me.

I just love chicken nuggets and chips to eat,

And sometimes cakes for a treat.

Red and blue are colours I like a lot,

My Chase, Marshall and Rubble and PAW Patrol toys are the best presents I ever got.

My favourite people are Mummy and Daddy, who are gems,

So this, my first poem, is just for them!

Ruben John Royston (3)

Foulsham & Bintree Playgroup, Dereham

My First Poem

My name is **Harley** and I go to preschool,

My best friend is **Emilia**, who is really cool.

I watch **Peppa Pig** on TV,

Playing **dinosaurs** is lots of fun for me.

I just love **chicken nuggets and chips** to eat,

And sometimes **lots of chocolate** for a treat.

Red is a colour I like a lot,

My **T-rex** is the best present I ever got.

My favourite person is **my mummy**, who is a gem,

So this, my first poem, is just for them!

Harley Wiseman-Marshall (3)

Foulsham & Bintree Playgroup, Dereham

My First Poem

My name is Finley and I go to preschool,

My best friend is Ruben, who is really cool.

I watch Scooby-Doo and PAW Patrol on TV,

Playing outside with my cars and trains is lots
of fun for me.

I just love lasagne and custard to eat,

And sometimes chocolate coins for a treat.

Red is a colour I like a lot,

My balance bike is the best present I ever got.

My favourite people are Mummy and Daddy, who
are gems,

So this, my first poem, is just for them!

Finley Rourke (3)
Foulsham & Bintree Playgroup, Dereham

My First Poem

My name is **Bethany** and I go to preschool,

My best friend is **Darcie**, who is really cool.

I watch **Stick Man** on TV,

Playing **with Play-Doh** is lots of fun for me.

I just love **cheese** to eat,

And sometimes **a bit of chocolate** for a treat.

Blue is a colour I like a lot,

My **kitchen and play food** are the best presents I ever got.

My favourite people are **my family**, who are gems,

So this, my first poem, is just for them!

Bethany Leeder (2)

Foulsham & Bintree Playgroup, Dereham

My First Poem

My name is Emilia and I go to preschool,

My best friend is Harley, who is really cool.

I watch Bing on TV,

Playing in the garden is lots of fun for me.

I just love Dunkers to eat,

And sometimes chocolate for a treat.

Blue is a colour I like a lot,

My bike is the best present I ever got.

My favourite person is Nanny 2, who is a gem,

So this, my first poem, is just for them!

Emilia Allen (2)

Foulsham & Bintree Playgroup, Dereham

My First Poem

My name is Harvey and I go to preschool,

My best friend is Hannah, who is really cool.

I watch Peppa Pig on TV,

Playing outside is lots of fun for me.

I just love apples to eat,

And sometimes sweets for a treat.

Blue is a colour I like a lot,

My wheelbarrow is the best present I ever got.

My favourite person is Daddy, who is a gem,

So this, my first poem, is just for them!

Harvey Patrick (2)

Foulsham & Bintree Playgroup, Dereham

My First Poem

My name is Leah and I go to preschool,

My best friend is Mummy, who is really cool.

I watch PAW Patrol on TV,

Playing spooky games is lots of fun for me.

I just love chicken and carrots to eat,

And sometimes chocolate cake for a treat.

Pink is a colour I like a lot,

My Lambie is the best present I ever got.

My favourite person is Mummy, who is a gem,

So this, my first poem, is just for them!

Leah Paige Westlake (3)
Foulsham & Bintree Playgroup, Dereham

My First Poem

My name is **Ellie** and I go to preschool,

My best friend is **Arianna**, who is really cool.

I watch **Peppa Pig and Frozen** on TV,

Playing **dressing up** is lots of fun for me.

I just love **potatoes** to eat,

And sometimes **sweets** for a treat.

Pink is a colour I like a lot,

My **fairy wand and wings** are the best presents I ever got.

My favourite person is **Adele**, who is a gem,

So this, my first poem, is just for them!

Ellie Chinn (3)

Foulsham & Bintree Playgroup, Dereham

My First Poem

My name is **Tia** and I go to preschool,

My best friend is **Roman**, who is really cool.

I watch **Horrid Henry** on TV,

Playing **with my dollies** is lots of fun for me.

I just love **beans** to eat,

And sometimes **chocolate** for a treat.

Red is a colour I like a lot,

My **dolly** is the best present I ever got.

My favourite person is **Grandma**, who is a gem,

So this, my first poem, is just for them!

Tia Porter (4)

Giggles Of Lytham, Lytham St Annes

My First Poem

My name is Sophia and I go to preschool,
My best friend is Armenia, who is really cool.
I watch Sofia the First on TV,
Playing with Barbies is lots of fun for me.
I just love spaghetti Bolognese to eat,
And sometimes chocolate for a treat.
Blue is a colour I like a lot,
My Frozen bike is the best present I ever got.
My favourite person is my sister, Alexa, who is a gem,
So this, my first poem, is just for them!

Sophia Alexa Taylor (4)

Giggles Of Lytham, Lytham St Annes

68

My First Poem

My name is Meher and I go to preschool,

My best friends are Lydia and Telissa, who are

really cool.

I watch movies on TV,

Playing with my train track is lots of fun for me.

I just love oranges to eat,

And sometimes yoghurt for a treat.

Green is a colour I like a lot,

My yo-yo is the best present I ever got.

My favourite person is Granny, who is a gem,

So this, my first poem, is just for them!

Meher Diwaker (4)

Giggles Of Lytham, Lytham St Annes

My First Poem

My name is Ruby and I go to preschool,

My best friend is Isla, who is really cool.

I watch Frozen on TV,

Playing Hungry Hippos is lots of fun for me.

I just love fish fingers to eat,

And sometimes chocolate for a treat.

Red is a colour I like a lot,

My singing Elsa is the best present I ever got.

My favourite person is Mummy, who is a gem,

So this, my first poem, is just for them!

Ruby Olivia Hibbert (3)

Giggles Of Lytham, Lytham St Annes

My First Poem

My name is Emily and I go to preschool,
My best friend is Sophia, who is really cool.
I watch Sooty on TV,
Playing with jigsaws is lots of fun for me.
I just love spaghetti soup to eat,
And sometimes chocolate for a treat.
Purple is a colour I like a lot,
My skateboard is the best present I ever got.
My favourite person is my sister, who is a gem,
So this, my first poem, is just for them!

Emily Southworth (4)
Giggles Of Lytham, Lytham St Annes

My First Poem

My name is Riley and I go to preschool,

My best friend is Ben, who is really cool.

I watch Power Rangers on TV,

Playing football is lots of fun for me.

I just love pasta bake to eat,

And sometimes chocolate for a treat.

Brown is a colour I like a lot,

My Iron Man costume is the best present I ever got.

My favourite person is Lexie, who is a gem,

So this, my first poem, is just for them!

Riley James Nicholson (4)

Giggles Of Lytham, Lytham St Annes

My First Poem

My name is Pixie and I go to preschool,
My best friend is Reggie, who is really cool.
I watch Frozen on TV,
Playing jigsaw is lots of fun for me.
I just love curry to eat,
And sometimes a lolly for a treat.
Purple is a colour I like a lot,
My bike is the best present I ever got.
My favourite person is Daddy, who is a gem,
So this, my first poem, is just for them!

Pixie Margaret Leaver (4)
Giggles Of Lytham, Lytham St Annes

My First Poem

My name is **Ben** and I go to preschool,

My best friend is **Riley**, who is really cool.

I watch **Dino Dan** on TV,

Playing **superheroes** is lots of fun for me.

I just love **sausages** to eat,

And sometimes **Haribo** for a treat.

Green is a colour I like a lot,

My **T-rex** is the best present I ever got.

My favourite person is **Granpa**, who is a gem,

So this, my first poem, is just for them!

Ben Flood (4)

Giggles Of Lytham, Lytham St Annes

My First Poem

My name is Leo and I go to preschool,

My best friend is Sophia, who is really cool.

I watch Charlie and Lola on TV,

Playing car showrooms is lots of fun for me.

I just love pizza to eat,

And sometimes chocolate for a treat.

Pink is a colour I like a lot,

My Lotus is the best present I ever got.

My favourite person is Granny, who is a gem,

So this, my first poem, is just for them!

Leo White (4)

Giggles Of Lytham, Lytham St Annes

My First Poem

My name is **Riley** and I go to preschool,

My best friend is **Issac**, who is really cool.

I watch **Dinosaurs** on TV,

Playing **with my Ninjago Lego** is lots of fun for me.

I just love **blueberries** to eat,

And sometimes **sweets** for a treat.

Red is a colour I like a lot,

My **football Lego** is the best present I ever got.

My favourite person is **Daddy**, who is a gem,

So this, my first poem, is just for them!

Riley Downes (3)

Happy Jacks Day Nursery, Littleborough

My First Poem

My name is Louis and I go to preschool,
My best friends are Miles and Grayson, who are
really cool.
I watch Dennis the Menace on TV,
Playing jigsaws is lots of fun for me.
I just love pies to eat,
And sometimes sweets and chocolate for a treat.
Red is a colour I like a lot,
My dinosaurs are the best presents I ever got.
My favourite person is Charlie, who is a gem,
So this, my first poem, is just for them!

Louis John Philip Braund (3)

Happy Jacks Day Nursery, Littleborough

My First Poem

My name is Leo and I go to preschool,

My best friends are Luc and Georgie, who are

really cool.

I watch Mike the Knight on TV,

Playing superheroes is lots of fun for me.

I just love chocolate to eat,

And sometimes we go swimming for a treat.

Blue is a colour I like a lot,

My Buzz Lightyear is the best present I ever got.

My favourite people are, all of my family,

they are gems,

So this, my first poem, is just for them!

Leo Giddins
Happy Jacks Day Nursery, Littleborough

My First Poem

My name is Khaleesi and I go to preschool,

My best friends are Grayson, Josh and Isaac, who
are really cool.

I watch Power Rangers on TV,

Playing football is lots of fun for me.

I just love fish fingers to eat,

And sometimes chocolate Mini Rolls for a treat.

Pink is a colour I like a lot,

My purple Happy Jacks hoodie is the best present
I ever got.

My favourite person is Caileb, my brother, who is
a gem,

So this, my first poem, is just for them!

Khaleesi Sharon Lorna Carroll (3)
Happy Jacks Day Nursery, Littleborough

My First Poem

My name is Ruby and I go to preschool,

My best friend is Miles, who is really cool.

I watch Peppa Pig on TV,

Playing tea parties is lots of fun for me.

I just love pasta to eat,

And sometimes strawberries for a treat.

Pink is a colour I like a lot,

My dolly pram is the best present I ever got.

My favourite person is Grandad, who is a gem,

So this, my first poem, is just for them!

Ruby Marie Gooding (2)

Happy Jacks Day Nursery, Littleborough

My First Poem

My name is Isabelle and I go to preschool,
My best friend is Jess, who is really cool.
I watch Yoga on TV,
Playing dollies is lots of fun for me.
I just love pizza to eat,
And sometimes biscuits for a treat.
Pink is a colour I like a lot,
My baby doll is the best present I ever got.
My favourite person is Thomas, who is a gem,
So this, my first poem, is just for them!

Isabelle Bostock (3)

Happy Jacks Day Nursery, Littleborough

My First Poem

My name is Skye and I go to preschool,

My best friend is Jessica, who is really cool.

I watch Peppa Pig on TV,

Playing with dollies and Play-Doh is lots of fun

for me.

I just love sandwiches and pizza to eat,

And sometimes a chocolate Kinder Surprise egg

for a treat.

Green is a colour I like a lot,

My toy supermarket is the best present I ever got.

My favourite person is Annabella, who is a gem,

So this, my first poem, is just for them!

Skye Ellouise Parsons (3)

Happy Jacks Day Nursery, Littleborough

My First Poem

My name is **Kristoff** and I go to preschool,

My best friend is **Jantzen**, who is really cool.

I watch **Timmy Time and Teletubbies** on TV,

Playing **choo choo trains and snakes** is lots of fun
for me.

I just love **hot dogs, ketchup and yoghurts**
to eat,

And sometimes **chocolate** for a treat.

Red is a colour I like a lot,

My **quad bike** is the best present I ever got.

My favourite person is **Mummy**, who is a gem,

So this, my first poem, is just for them!

Kristoff White Ogu (2)

Happy Jacks Day Nursery, Littleborough

83

My First Poem

My name is Miles and I go to preschool,

My best friend is Grayson, who is really cool.

I watch Batman on TV,

Playing superheroes with Grayson is lots of fun

for me.

I just love sausages to eat,

And sometimes ice cream for a treat.

Blue is a colour I like a lot,

My Batman cape is the best present I ever got.

My favourite person is Mummy, who is a gem,

So this, my first poem, is just for them!

Miles Parfitt (2)

Happy Jacks Day Nursery, Littleborough

My First Poem

My name is **Brandon** and I go to preschool,

My best friends are **Michelle and Rachael**, who are really cool.

I watch **PAW Patrol** on TV,

Playing **on my scooter** is lots of fun for me.

I just love **beans, chicken nuggets and ketchup** to eat,

And sometimes **cake** for a treat.

Pink is a colour I like a lot,

My **bike** is the best present I ever got.

My favourite person is **Nanna**, who is a gem,

So this, my first poem, is just for them!

Brandon Lee Brooks (3)

Happy Jacks Day Nursery, Littleborough

My First Poem

My name is Grayson and I go to preschool,

My best friends are Harvey and Edward, who

are really cool.

I watch CBeebies and superheroes on TV,

Playing with sticker books and Lego is lots of fun

for me.

I just love ham sandwiches to eat,

And sometimes chocolate biscuits for a treat.

Green is a colour I like a lot,

My rugby hat is the best present I ever got.

My favourite person is Granny Janny, who is a gem,

So this, my first poem, is just for them!

Grayson Howard (3)

Happy Jacks Day Nursery, Littleborough

My First Poem

My name is Isabelle and I go to preschool,
My best friend is Isla, who is really cool.
I watch PAW Patrol on TV,
Playing with Tilly is lots of fun for me.
I just love macaroni cheese to eat,
And sometimes chocolate for a treat.
Pink is a colour I like a lot,
My scooter is the best present I ever got.
My favourite person is Mummy, who is a gem,
So this, my first poem, is just for them!

Isabelle Sparkes (4)
Happylands Private Day Nursery, Wardon

My First Poem

My name is **Tobias** and I go to preschool,

My best friend is **Connie**, who is really cool.

I watch **Dinosaur Adventure** on TV,

Playing **on the computer at preschool** is lots of

fun for me.

I just love **pizza and porridge** to eat,

And sometimes **cake** for a treat.

Blue is a colour I like a lot,

My **new bike** is the best present I ever got.

My favourite person is **Mummy**, who is a gem,

So this, my first poem, is just for them!

Tobias Schatzberger (3)

Humshaugh & District Preschool, Hexham

My First Poem

My name is Callum and I go to preschool,

My best friend is Sophie, who is really cool.

I watch PAW Patrol and Dora and Friends on TV,

Playing tag, tractors and playing with Mummy are lots of fun for me.

I just love pizza and pasta to eat,

And sometimes cereal for a treat.

Blue is a colour I like a lot,

My squirty flower is the best present I ever got.

My favourite person is Mummy, who is a gem,

So this, my first poem, is just for them!

Callum Wood (4)

Humshaugh & District Preschool, Hexham

My First Poem

My name is **Teddy** and I go to preschool,

My best friend is **Max**, who is really cool.

I watch **Ghostbusters** on TV,

Playing **Lego Marvel's Avengers** is lots of fun

for me.

I just love **pizza** to eat,

And sometimes **ice cream and biscuits** for a treat.

Red is a colour I like a lot,

My **new Hulk Buster** is the best present I ever got.

My favourite person is **my dad**, who is a gem,

So this, my first poem, is just for them!

Teddy James McKenzie (3)

Humshaugh & District Preschool, Hexham

My First Poem

My name is Mia and I go to preschool,

My best friend is Ellie, who is really cool.

I watch PAW Patrol on TV,

Playing the cow game on the computer is lots of

fun for me.

I just love snacks to eat,

And sometimes breadsticks for a treat.

Blue is a colour I like a lot,

My Barbie car is the best present I ever got.

My favourite person is Mummy, who is a gem,

So this, my first poem, is just for them!

Mia Robinson (3)
Humshaugh & District Preschool, Hexham

My First Poem

My name is Winston and I go to preschool,

My best friend is Alex, who is really cool.

I watch Batman on TV,

Playing with cars is lots of fun for me.

I just love spaghetti Bolognese to eat,

And sometimes sweeties for a treat.

Blue is a colour I like a lot,

My Iron Man is the best present I ever got.

My favourite people are Mummy and Daddy, who
are gems,

So this, my first poem, is just for them!

Winston Richards (3)

Little Oaks Day Nursery, Newcastle

My First Poem

My name is **Sebastian** and I go to preschool,
My best friend is **Winston**, who is really cool.
I watch **PAW Patrol** on TV,
Playing **dinosaurs** is lots of fun for me.
I just love **waffles and beans** to eat,
And sometimes **sweets** for a treat.
Green is a colour I like a lot,
My **cars** are the best presents I ever got.
My favourite person is **Mummy**, who is a gem,
So this, my first poem, is just for them!

Sebastian Harris (3)

Little Oaks Day Nursery, Newcastle

My First Poem

My name is Everleigh and I go to preschool,

My best friend is Amber, who is really cool.

I watch The Hunger Games on TV,

Playing with my doll's house is lots of fun for me.

I just love beans on toast to eat,

And sometimes McDonald's for a treat.

Pink, yellow and red are colours I like a lot,

My singing Barbie is the best present I ever got.

My favourite people are Mummy and Daddy, who

are gems,

So this, my first poem, is just for them!

Everleigh Tomlinson (3)

Little Oaks Day Nursery, Newcastle

My First Poem

My name is Jan and I go to preschool,

My best friend is Alexander, who is really cool.

I watch Postman Pat on TV,

Playing cars is lots of fun for me.

I just love pasta to eat,

And sometimes lollipops for a treat.

Blue is a colour I like a lot,

My Batman is the best present I ever got.

My favourite person is Marta, who is a gem,

So this, my first poem, is just for them!

Jan Choina (3)

Little Oaks Day Nursery, Newcastle

My First Poem

My name is Hope and I go to preschool,

My best friend is Mummy, who is really cool.

I watch Peppa Pig on TV,

Playing and colouring are lots of fun for me.

I just love cookies to eat,

And sometimes chocolate bars for a treat.

Pink is a colour I like a lot,

My Minnie Mouse is the best present I ever got.

My favourite person is baby Lily, who is a gem,

So this, my first poem, is just for them!

Hope Elizabeth Evans (3)

Little Oaks Day Nursery, Newcastle

My First Poem

My name is Alexander and I go to preschool,
My best friend is Winston, who is really cool.
I watch Minions on TV,
Playing with cars is lots of fun for me.
I just love spaghetti to eat,
And sometimes a Kinder Surprise egg for a treat.
Pink is a colour I like a lot,
My big Transformer car is the best present I
ever got.
My favourite person is Daddy, who is a gem,
So this, my first poem, is just for them!

Alexander Wyrwa (3)

Little Oaks Day Nursery, Newcastle

My First Poem

My name is Samar and I go to preschool,

My best friend is Alexander, who is really cool.

I watch Peppa Pig on TV,

Playing with my doll's house is lots of fun for me.

I just love vegetables to eat,

And sometimes a new toy for a treat.

Red is a colour I like a lot,

My cars are the best presents I ever got.

My favourite person is Mummy, who is a gem,

So this, my first poem, is just for them!

Samar Singh Zandu (3)

Little Oaks Day Nursery, Newcastle

My First Poem

My name is Riley and I go to preschool,

My best friend is Winston, who is really cool.

I watch Lion King on TV,

Playing with cars is lots of fun for me.

I just love toast to eat,

And sometimes chocolate for a treat.

Blue is a colour I like a lot,

My big car truck is the best present I ever got.

My favourite person is my mummy, who is a gem,

So this, my first poem, is just for them!

Riley Barnett (3)

Little Oaks Day Nursery, Newcastle

My First Poem

My name is Maxi and I go to preschool,

My best friend is my daddy, who is really cool.

I watch cartoons on TV,

Playing with cars is lots of fun for me.

I just love pasta and vegetables to eat,

And sometimes chocolate for a treat.

Green is a colour I like a lot,

My toys are the best presents I ever got.

My favourite person is Cooper, who is a gem,

So this, my first poem, is just for them!

Maxi Clews (4)

Little Oaks Day Nursery, Newcastle

My First Poem

My name is Heidi and I go to preschool,

My best friend is Amber, who is really cool.

I watch Peppa Pig on TV,

Playing with my kitchen is lots of fun for me.

I just love spaghetti to eat,

And sometimes ice cream for a treat.

Pink is a colour I like a lot,

My Peppa Pig bobbles are the best present I

ever got.

My favourite person is Emily, who is a gem,

So this, my first poem, is just for them!

Heidi Sharp (3)
Little Oaks Day Nursery, Newcastle

My First Poem

My name is **Amber** and I go to preschool,

My best friend is **Heidi**, who is really cool.

I watch **Peppa Pig** on TV,

Playing **princesses** is lots of fun for me.

I just love **pasta** to eat,

And sometimes **cake** for a treat.

Pink is a colour I like a lot,

My **Frozen toy** is the best present I ever got.

My favourite person is **Mummy**, who is a gem,

So this, my first poem, is just for them!

Amber Badu (3)

Little Oaks Day Nursery, Newcastle

My First Poem

My name is Davi and I go to preschool,

My best friend is Lachlan, who is really cool.

I watch Thomas and Friends on TV,

Playing with toys is lots of fun for me.

I just love pizza to eat,

And sometimes sweeties for a treat.

Blue is a colour I like a lot,

My car is the best present I ever got.

My favourite person is Daddy, who is a gem,

So this, my first poem, is just for them!

Davi Esteves (3)

Little Scallywags Ltd, Crieff

My First Poem

My name is Lachlan and I go to preschool,

My best friend is Dylan, who is really cool.

I watch Lego men on TV,

Playing and drawing are lots of fun for me.

I just love apples to eat,

And sometimes sweeties for a treat.

Red is a colour I like a lot,

My Lego truck is the best present I ever got.

My favourite person is Mummy, who is a gem,

So this, my first poem, is just for them!

Lachlan Stewart (3)

Little Scallywags Ltd, Crieff

My First Poem

My name is Dylan and I go to preschool,

My best friend is Lachlan, who is really cool.

I watch PAW Patrol on TV,

Playing with a big truck is lots of fun for me.

I just love yoghurt to eat,

And sometimes ice cream for a treat.

Blue is a colour I like a lot,

My bike is the best present I ever got.

My favourite person is Mummy, who is a gem,

So this, my first poem, is just for them!

Dylan Rennie (3)

Little Scallywags Ltd, Crieff

My First Poem

My name is Elizabeth and I go to preschool,

My best friend is Freya, who is really cool.

I watch Peppa Pig on TV,

Playing house is lots of fun for me.

I just love eggs to eat,

And sometimes sweets for a treat.

Pink is a colour I like a lot,

My Sylvanian house is the best present I ever got.

My favourite people are Mummy and Daddy, who

are gems,

So this, my first poem, is just for them!

Elizabeth Mary Pearse (4)

Metheringham Preschool, Lincoln

My First Poem

My name is Ella and I go to preschool,

My best friend is Freya, who is really cool.

I watch PAW Patrol on TV,

Playing on the slide is lots of fun for me.

I just love apples to eat,

And sometimes a lolly for a treat.

Pink is a colour I like a lot,

My Rapunzel is the best present I ever got.

My favourite person is Mum, who is a gem,

So this, my first poem, is just for them!

Ella May Reed (4)

Metheringham Preschool, Lincoln

My First Poem

My name is **Harley** and I go to preschool,

My best friend is **Jenson**, who is really cool.

I watch **CBeebies** on TV,

Playing **Captain Tim** is lots of fun for me.

I just love **chicken** to eat,

And sometimes **sweeties** for a treat.

Blue is a colour I like a lot,

My **car** is the best present I ever got.

My favourite person is **Mummy**, who is a gem,

So this, my first poem, is just for them!

Harley Kye Redden (3)
Muddy Boots Preschool, Northampton

My First Poem

My name is Ellis and I go to preschool,

My best friend is Lily, who is really cool.

I watch PAW Patrol on TV,

Playing dressing up is lots of fun for me.

I just love strawberries to eat,

And sometimes ice cream for a treat.

White is a colour I like a lot,

My birdies are the best present I ever got.

My favourite person is Mummy, who is a gem,

So this, my first poem, is just for them!

Ellis Middleton-Hale (3)
Muddy Boots Preschool, Northampton

My First Poem

My name is **Kobie** and I go to preschool,

My best friend is **Toby**, who is really cool.

I watch **Peppa Pig** on TV,

Playing **with trains** is lots of fun for me.

I just love **Cheerios** to eat,

And sometimes **chocolate** for a treat.

Purple is a colour I like a lot,

My **cars** are the best presents I ever got.

My favourite person is **Mummy**, who is a gem,

So this, my first poem, is just for them!

Kobie Loveridge (3)

Muddy Boots Preschool, Northampton

My First Poem

My name is **Toby** and I go to preschool,

My best friend is **Tommy**, who is really cool.

I watch **PAW Patrol** on TV,

Playing **dragons** is lots of fun for me.

I just love **sweetcorn** to eat,

And sometimes **ice cream** for a treat.

Red is a colour I like a lot,

My **Marshall with a ladder** is the best present I
ever got.

My favourite people are **Mummy and Daddy**, who
are gems,

So this, my first poem, is just for them!

Toby Evans (4)
Muddy Boots Preschool, Northampton

My First Poem

My name is Jack and I go to preschool,

My best friend is George, who is really cool.

I watch Curious George on TV,

Playing with my lawn mower is lots of fun for me.

I just love cheese on toast to eat,

And sometimes chocolate for a treat.

Green is a colour I like a lot,

My tool set is the best present I ever got.

My favourite people are Mummy and Daddy, who

are gems,

So this, my first poem, is just for them!

Jack Cobain Davies (4)

Muddy Boots Preschool, Northampton

My First Poem

My name is Ollie and I go to preschool,

My best friend is Tommy, who is really cool.

I watch Peppa Pig on TV,

Playing with cars is lots of fun for me.

I just love spaghetti to eat,

And sometimes chocolate for a treat.

Blue is a colour I like a lot,

My remote control car is the best present I

ever got.

My favourite person is Mummy, who is a gem,

So this, my first poem, is just for them!

Ollie Clarke (4)

Muddy Boots Preschool, Northampton

My First Poem

My name is Evie and I go to preschool,

My best friend is Leila, who is really cool.

I watch Peppa Pig on TV,

Playing babies is lots of fun for me.

I just love pasta to eat,

And sometimes bread for a treat.

Orange is a colour I like a lot,

My Peppa Pig is the best present I ever got.

My favourite person is Meme, who is a gem,

So this, my first poem, is just for them!

Evie Miller (3)
Muddy Boots Preschool, Northampton

My First Poem

My name is Lily and I go to preschool,

My best friend is Tommy, who is really cool.

I watch Spider-Man and Rapunzel on TV,

Playing with my Peppa Pig house is lots of fun

for me.

I just love chicken to eat,

And sometimes chocolate for a treat.

Red is a colour I like a lot,

My roller skates are the best present I ever got.

My favourite person is Daddy, who is a gem,

So this, my first poem, is just for them!

Lily Rose Quigley (4)

Muddy Boots Preschool, Northampton

My First Poem

My name is Molly and I go to preschool,

My best friend is Ollie, who is really cool.

I watch Peppa Pig on TV,

Playing dinosaurs is lots of fun for me.

I just love chocolate cake to eat,

And sometimes I have sweeties for a treat.

Orange is a colour I like a lot,

My wind up dinosaur is the best present I ever got.

My favourite person is Tommy, who is a gem,

So this, my first poem, is just for them!

Molly Tillett (4)

Muddy Boots Preschool, Northampton

My First Poem

My name is Lily and I go to preschool,

My best friend is Ellis, who is really cool.

I watch Peppa Pig on TV,

Playing kitchens and dressing up are lots of fun

for me.

I just love pasta to eat,

And sometimes sweeties for a treat.

Pink is a colour I like a lot,

My Barbie is the best present I ever got.

My favourite person is Ellis, who is a gem,

So this, my first poem, is just for them!

Lily Downer (3)
Muddy Boots Preschool, Northampton

117

My First Poem

My name is **Emmeline** and I go to preschool,

My best friend is **Marlie**, who is really cool.

I watch **PAW Patrol** on TV,

Playing **on my iPad and with Lucy, my cat**, is lots of fun for me.

I just love **pasta** to eat,

And sometimes **sweets** for a treat.

Blue is a colour I like a lot,

My **Frozen characters** are the best presents I ever got.

My favourite person is **Betsy**, who is a gem,

So this, my first poem, is just for them!

Emmeline Violet Moore (4)

Muddy Boots Preschool, Northampton

My First Poem

My name is Marlie and I go to preschool,

My best friend is Emmeline, who is really cool.

I watch Blaze and the Monster Machines
on TV,

Playing with my mini puzzle is lots of fun for me.

I just love meatballs and pizza to eat,

And sometimes I get a cake with a cherry on top
for a treat.

Pink is a colour I like a lot,

My panda is the best present I ever got.

My favourite person is Mummy, who is a gem,

So this, my first poem, is just for them!

Marlie Florence Chelsey Ellaby (3)
Muddy Boots Preschool, Northampton

My First Poem

My name is Jenson and I go to preschool,

My best friend is Molly, who is really cool.

I watch Cars movie on TV,

Playing dressing up is lots of fun for me.

I just love pizza to eat,

And sometimes I get an ice cream for a treat.

Rainbow colours are colours I like a lot,

My toy caravan is the best present I ever got.

My favourite person is Mummy, who is a gem,

So this, my first poem, is just for them!

Jenson Budd (4)
Muddy Boots Preschool, Northampton

My First Poem

My name is **Harry** and I go to preschool,

My best friend is **Tommy**, who is really cool.

I watch **Fireman Sam** on TV,

Playing **with my Octonauts** is lots of fun for me.

I just love **pizza** to eat,

And sometimes **cake** for a treat.

Green is a colour I like a lot,

My **Octonaut** is the best present I ever got.

My favourite person is **Nanny**, who is a gem,

So this, my first poem, is just for them!

Harry Sweeney (2)

Muddy Boots Preschool, Northampton

My First Poem

My name is Leila and I go to preschool,
My best friend is Indi, who is really cool.
I watch Peppa Pig on TV,
Playing dressing up is lots of fun for me.
I just love pasta and sauce to eat,
And sometimes cake for a treat.
Orange is a colour I like a lot,
My hairdryer is the best present I ever got.
My favourite person is Daddy, who is a gem,
So this, my first poem, is just for them!

Leila Leonard (4)
Muddy Boots Preschool, Northampton

My First Poem

My name is Lucy and I go to preschool,

My best friend is Ben, who is really cool.

I watch Ben & Holly on TV,

Playing cooking is lots of fun for me.

I just love cheese sandwiches and
tomato soup to eat,

And sometimes chocolate for a treat.

Pink is a colour I like a lot,

My fairy castle and fairy are the best presents I
ever got.

My favourite person is Mummy, who is a gem,

So this, my first poem, is just for them!

Lucy Burchell (3)

Muddy Boots Preschool, Northampton

My First Poem

My name is Jack and I go to preschool,

My best friend is Tyler, who is really cool.

I watch Mike the Knight on TV,

Playing and painting are lots of fun for me.

I just love jam on toast to eat,

And sometimes chocolate for a treat.

Blue is a colour I like a lot,

My goal and football are the best presents I

ever got.

My favourite person is Mummy, who is a gem,

So this, my first poem, is just for them!

Jack Hudson-Pridmore (3)

Muddy Boots Preschool, Northampton

My First Poem

My name is Teagan and I go to preschool,

My best friend is Harley, who is really cool.

I watch Peppa Pig on TV,

Playing Peppa Pig is lots of fun for me.

I just love toast to eat,

And sometimes chicken nuggets for a treat.

Red is a colour I like a lot,

My Peppa Pig is the best present I ever got.

My favourite person is Mummy, who is a gem,

So this, my first poem, is just for them!

Teagan Linnell (2)

Muddy Boots Preschool, Northampton

My First Poem

My name is Dylan and I go to preschool,

My best friend is Jack, who is really cool.

I watch Octonauts on TV,

Playing Octonauts is lots of fun for me.

I just love Coco Pops to eat,

And sometimes chocolate for a treat.

Pink is a colour I like a lot,

My Minions are the best present I ever got.

My favourite person is Dexter, who is a gem,

So this, my first poem, is just for them!

Dylan Feasey (4)

Muddy Boots Preschool, Northampton

My First Poem

My name is Blake and I go to preschool,

My best friend is Leo, who is really cool.

I watch Pingu on TV,

Playing with cars is lots of fun for me.

I just love cheese to eat,

And sometimes chocolate for a treat.

Green is a colour I like a lot,

My remote control car is the best present I

ever got.

My favourite people are the preschool teachers,

who are gems,

So this, my first poem, is just for them!

Blake Peter Noel Boulter (3)

Muddy Boots Preschool, Northampton

My First Poem

My name is Ted and I go to preschool,

My best friend is Kobie, who is really cool.

I watch Thomas the Tank Engine on TV,

Playing with dragon toys is lots of fun for me.

I just love chips to eat,

And sometimes chocolate for a treat.

Red and blue are colours I like a lot,

My Spider-Man is the best present I ever got.

My favourite people are my brothers, who are gems,

So this, my first poem, is just for them!

Ted Murray (3)

Muddy Boots Preschool, Northampton

My First Poem

My name is Tommy and I go to preschool,
My best friend is Lily, who is really cool.
I watch Kung Fu Panda on TV,
Playing superheroes is lots of fun for me.
I just love pasta to eat,
And sometimes sweeties and chocolate cake for
a treat.
Blue is a colour I like a lot,
My Mashers Superheroes are the best presents I
ever got.
My favourite people are Ollie and Jess, who are gems,
So this, my first poem, is just for them!

Tommy Jeffery (4)
Muddy Boots Preschool, Northampton

My First Poem

My name is Oscar and I go to preschool,

My best friend is Molly, who is really cool.

I watch Choo Choo on TV,

Playing with trains is lots of fun for me.

I just love toast to eat,

And sometimes Jelly Babies for a treat.

Blue is a colour I like a lot,

My trains are the best presents I ever got.

My favourite people are Mummy and Daddy, who

are gems,

So this, my first poem, is just for them!

Oscar Benedetti (3)

Muddy Boots Preschool, Northampton

My First Poem

My name is Bowan and I go to preschool,

My best friend is Fraser, who is really cool.

I watch Minnie Mouse on TV,

Playing with my Minnie Mouse teddy is lots of fun for me.

I just love sausage and beans to eat,

And sometimes a lollipop for a treat.

Pink is a colour I like a lot,

My singing Minnie Mouse doll is the best present I ever got.

My favourite people are my mummies, who are gems,

So this, my first poem, is just for them!

Bowan Thomas-Wainwright (3)

Muddy Boots Preschool, Northampton

My First Poem

My name is **Mackenzie** and I go to preschool,

My best friend is **Lucie**, who is really cool.

I watch **Power Rangers** on TV,

Playing **BunBun at home** is lots of fun for me.

I just love **spaghetti Bolognese** to eat,

And sometimes **chocolate** for a treat.

Green is a colour I like a lot,

My **cake** is the best present I ever got.

My favourite person is **Lucie**, who is a gem,

So this, my first poem, is just for them!

Mackenzie Katie Thomas-Wainwright (4)

Muddy Boots Preschool, Northampton

My First Poem

My name is **Alfie** and I go to preschool,
My best friend is **Darcey**, who is really cool.
I watch **Peter Rabbit** on TV,
Playing **Batman** is lots of fun for me.
I just love **pizza** to eat,
And sometimes **sweeties** for a treat.
Red is a colour I like a lot,
My **PAW Patrol scooter** is the best present I
ever got.
My favourite person is **Daddy**, who is a gem,
So this, my first poem, is just for them!

Alfie Ebrey (3)
Napley Lodge Farm Day Nursery, Market Drayton

My First Poem

My name is Bonnie and I go to preschool,

My best friend is Izzy, who is really cool.

I watch Mr Bean on TV,

Playing with cars is lots of fun for me.

I just love pasta to eat,

And sometimes sweeties for a treat.

Blue is a colour I like a lot,

My Barbie car is the best present I ever got.

My favourite person is Mummy, who is a gem,

So this, my first poem, is just for them!

Bonnie Sadie Withers (3)

Peter Pan Preschool, Nuneaton

My First Poem

My name is Evie and I go to preschool,

My best friend is Arin, who is really cool.

I watch CBeebies on TV,

Playing with Barbies is lots of fun for me.

I just love sandwiches to eat,

And sometimes chocolate for a treat.

Yellow and blue are colours I like a lot,

My princess doll is the best present I ever got.

My favourite person is Nanny, who is a gem,

So this, my first poem, is just for them!

Evie McHugh (3)
Peter Pan Preschool, Nuneaton

My First Poem

My name is Kaytlin and I go to preschool,

My best friend is Issy, who is really cool.

I watch Teenage Mutant Ninja Turtles on TV,

Playing with squirting water toys is lots of fun

for me.

I just love pizza to eat,

And sometimes chocolate for a treat.

Pink is a colour I like a lot,

My watch from Nanny is the best present I ever got.

My favourite person is Daddy, who is a gem,

So this, my first poem, is just for them!

Kaytlin Elizabeth Bradford (4)

Peter Pan Preschool, Nuneaton

My First Poem

My name is Charlie and I go to preschool,

My best friend is Jack, who is really cool.

I watch Fireman Sam on TV,

Playing with cars is lots of fun for me.

I just love pizza to eat,

And sometimes chocolate for a treat.

Red is a colour I like a lot,

My Bumblebee is the best present I ever got.

My favourite person is Mummy, who is a gem,

So this, my first poem, is just for them!

Charlie Joe Briggs (3)

Peter Pan Preschool, Nuneaton

My First Poem

My name is Britanny and I go to preschool,

My best friend is Arin, who is really cool.

I watch Frozen on TV,

Playing with my house is lots of fun for me.

I just love spaghetti to eat,

And sometimes chocolate for a treat.

Pink is a colour I like a lot,

My Anna and Elsa are the best presents I ever got.

My favourite person is Chester, who is a gem,

So this, my first poem, is just for them!

Britanny Faith Bongayen Che (3)

Peter Pan Preschool, Nuneaton

My First Poem

My name is Teddy and I go to preschool,

My best friend is Arin, who is really cool.

I watch Mickey Mouse Clubhouse on TV,

Playing with my toy dinosaurs is lots of fun for me.

I just love raspberries and strawberries to eat,

And sometimes chocolate ice cream for a treat.

Purple is a colour I like a lot,

My Spider-Man Lego is the best present I ever got.

My favourite person is my brother, Isaac, who is

a gem,

So this, my first poem, is just for them!

Teddy Saul Twamley (3)

Peter Pan Preschool, Nuneaton

My First Poem

My name is **Tulisa** and I go to preschool,

My best friend is **Chloee**, who is really cool.

I watch **Frozen** on TV,

Playing **hide-and-seek** is lots of fun for me.

I just love **cucumber** to eat,

And sometimes **chocolate ice cream** for a treat.

Blue is a colour I like a lot,

My **scooter** is the best present I ever got.

My favourite person is **my daddy**, who is a gem,

So this, my first poem, is just for them!

Tulisa Ann Phythian (3)

Peter Pan Preschool, Nuneaton

My First Poem

My name is **Tiara Rai** and I go to preschool,

My best friend is **Serene**, who is really cool.

I watch **cartoons** on TV,

Playing **with bubble blower and sand** is lots of fun for me.

I just love **fruits** to eat,

And sometimes **chocolates** for a treat.

Pink is a colour I like a lot,

My **iPad** is the best present I ever got.

My favourite person is **my mummy**, who is a gem,

So this, my first poem, is just for them!

Tiara Rai (4)

Peter Pan Preschool, Nuneaton

My First Poem

My name is Jack and I go to preschool,

My best friend is Jenson, who is really cool.

I watch PAW Patrol on TV,

Playing aeroplanes is lots of fun for me.

I just love pizza to eat,

And sometimes sweeties for a treat.

Red is a colour I like a lot,

My car is the best present I ever got.

My favourite person is Mummy, who is a gem,

So this, my first poem, is just for them!

Jack Cairns (4)

Peter Pan Preschool, Nuneaton

My First Poem

My name is Max and I go to preschool,

My best friend is Dawson, who is really cool.

I watch PAW Patrol on TV,

Playing football is lots of fun for me.

I just love sausage and chips to eat,

And sometimes sweeties for a treat.

Green is a colour I like a lot,

My dragon is the best present I ever got.

My favourite people are Mummy, Oscar and Daddy, who are gems,

So this, my first poem, is just for them!

Max Bream (4)

Ravensmere Arc, Beccles

My First Poem

My name is Alice and I go to preschool,

My best friend is Tilly, who is really cool.

I watch Dora the Explorer on TV,

Playing board games is lots of fun for me.

I just love Weetabix to eat,

And sometimes chocolate for a treat.

Pink is a colour I like a lot,

My ted, the pink ted, is the best present I ever got.

My favourite person is Mummy, who is a gem,

So this, my first poem, is just for them!

Alice Olivia Hardy (3)

Ravensmere Arc, Beccles

My First Poem

My name is Ethan and I go to preschool,

My best friend is Mummy, who is really cool.

I watch PAW Patrol on TV,

Playing with cars is lots of fun for me.

I just love biscuits to eat,

And sometimes cakes for a treat.

Brown is a colour I like a lot,

My PAW Patrol tower is the best present I ever got.

My favourite person is Mummy, who is a gem,

So this, my first poem, is just for them!

Ethan Masterson (3)

Ravensmere Arc, Beccles

My First Poem

My name is Tilly and I go to preschool,

My best friend is Millie, who is really cool.

I watch Peppa Pig on TV,

Playing with Play-Doh is lots of fun for me.

I just love sausages to eat,

And sometimes sweets for a treat.

Purple is a colour I like a lot,

My Peppa Pig headphones are the best present I

ever got.

My favourite person is my sister, Molly, who is a gem,

So this, my first poem, is just for them!

Tilly Turner (3)

Ravensmere Arc, Beccles

My First Poem

My name is Esme and I go to preschool,

My best friend is my big sister, Ruby, who is

really cool.

I watch Peppa Pig and Disney Junior on TV,

Playing jumping around in muddy puddles is

lots of fun for me.

I just love grapes to eat,

And sometimes chocolate for a treat.

Pink is a colour I like a lot,

My bedroom being decorated is the best present

I ever got.

My favourite person is Mummy, who is a gem,

So this, my first poem, is just for them!

Esme Pitts (3)

Ravensmere Arc, Beccles

My First Poem

My name is Joe and I go to preschool,

My best friend is Ethan, who is really cool.

I watch Octonauts on TV,

Playing with cars is lots of fun for me.

I just love raisins and dates to eat,

And sometimes chocolate for a treat.

Blue is a colour I like a lot,

My Hot Wheels are the best presents I ever got.

My favourite person is James, my cousin, who is

a gem,

So this, my first poem, is just for them!

Joe Worlledge (3)

Ravensmere Arc, Beccles

My First Poem

My name is Emment and I go to preschool,

My best friend is Flynn, who is really cool.

I watch Umizoomi on TV,

Playing with Play-Doh is lots of fun for me.

I just love apples to eat,

And sometimes Kinder eggs for a treat.

Blue is a colour I like a lot,

My Effie is the best present I ever got.

My favourite person is Mummy, who is a gem,

So this, my first poem, is just for them!

Emment Oddy (3)

Ravensmere Arc, Beccles

My First Poem

My name is **Poppy** and I go to preschool,

My best friend is **Amanda Hogkinson**, who is

really cool.

I watch **Mike the Knight** on TV,

Playing **with my dollies** is lots of fun for me.

I just love **sweets and chocolate** to eat,

And sometimes **trifle** for a treat.

Pink is a colour I like a lot,

My **scooter** is the best present I ever got.

My favourite person is **Hollie-Jayne**, who is a gem,

So this, my first poem, is just for them!

Poppy May Ambridge (2)

Seashells Nursery, Mablethorpe

My First Poem

My name is Kaitlyn and I go to preschool,
My best friend is Charles, who is really cool.
I watch Lego Friends on TV,
Playing and gluing are lots of fun for me.
I just love sausages to eat,
And sometimes Maltesers for a treat.
Pink is a colour I like a lot,
My colouring book is the best present I ever got.
My favourite person is Mummy, who is a gem,
So this, my first poem, is just for them!

Kaitlyn Betson (3)

Seashells Nursery, Mablethorpe

My First Poem

My name is Victoria and I go to preschool,

My best friend is Emily, who is really cool.

I watch Blaze and the Monster Machines on TV,

Playing Doggy Doo is lots of fun for me.

I just love hot dogs and broccoli to eat,

And sometimes a Kinder egg for a treat.

Hot pink is a colour I like a lot,

My Gooey Louie is the best present I ever got.

My favourite person is my sister, Megan, who is a gem,

So this, my first poem, is just for them!

Victoria Brown (4)

Seashells Nursery, Mablethorpe

My First Poem

My name is Mason and I go to preschool,

My best friend is Jacob, who is really cool.

I watch Dumbo on TV,

Playing with cars is lots of fun for me.

I just love sausages to eat,

And sometimes bananas for a treat.

Red is a colour I like a lot,

My quad is the best present I ever got.

My favourite person is my mummy, who is a gem,

So this, my first poem, is just for them!

Mason McCafferty (4)

Seashells Nursery, Mablethorpe

My First Poem

My name is **Xander** and I go to preschool,

My best friend is **Maisy**, who is really cool.

I watch **Mister Maker** on TV,

Playing **with my trains** is lots of fun for me.

I just love **doughnuts and fruit** to eat,

And sometimes **Kinder eggs** for a treat.

Black is a colour I like a lot,

My **rocky track and sports car** are the best

presents I ever got.

My favourite person is **Maisy**, who is a gem,

So this, my first poem, is just for them!

Xander Talen Windrass-Gibson (3)

Seashells Nursery, Mablethorpe

My First Poem

My name is Lydia and I go to preschool,
My best friend is Grandad, who is really cool.
I watch Toy Story on TV,
Playing with dolls is lots of fun for me.
I just love chicken to eat,
And sometimes ice cream for a treat.
Red is a colour I like a lot,
My Baby Annabell doll is the best present I ever got.
My favourite person is Grandad, who is a gem,
So this, my first poem, is just for them!

Lydia Allsop (3)

Seashells Nursery, Mablethorpe

My First Poem

My name is Isabella and I go to preschool,

My best friend is Caitlyn, who is really cool.

I watch Peppa Pig on TV,

Playing babies with Rylie is lots of fun for me.

I just love chicken nuggets to eat,

And sometimes sweets for a treat.

Blue, brown and white are colours I like a lot,

My electric scooter is the best present I ever got.

My favourite person is Daddy, who is a gem,

So this, my first poem, is just for them!

Isabella Bowmar (3)

Seashells Nursery, Mablethorpe

My First Poem

My name is Shay and I go to preschool,
My best friend is Daddy, who is really cool.
I watch Beauty and the Beast on TV,
Playing with my kitchen is lots of fun for me.
I just love cheese to eat,
And sometimes an ice lolly for a treat.
Pink is a colour I like a lot,
My monkey is the best present I ever got.
My favourite person is my mummy, who is a gem,
So this, my first poem, is just for them!

Shay Dane (3)
Seashells Nursery, Mablethorpe

My First Poem

My name is **Charlie** and I go to preschool,

My best friend is **Riley**, who is really cool.

I watch **SpongeBob SquarePants** on TV,

Playing **hide-and-seek** is lots of fun for me.

I just love **mashed potato** to eat,

And sometimes **ice cream** for a treat.

Blue is a colour I like a lot,

My **Anna doll** is the best present I ever got.

My favourite person is **my brother, Evan**, who is

a gem,

So this, my first poem, is just for them!

Charlie Stacey (3)

Seashells Nursery, Mablethorpe

My First Poem

My name is Emily and I go to preschool,

My best friend is Tilly, who is really cool.

I watch Ben & Holly's Little Kingdom on TV,

Playing with my toys is lots of fun for me.

I just love apples to eat,

And sometimes chocolate for a treat.

Blue is a colour I like a lot,

My Peppa Pig bed is the best present I ever got.

My favourite person is Sasha, who is a gem,

So this, my first poem, is just for them!

Emily Jesney (2)

Seashells Nursery, Mablethorpe

My First Poem

My name is **Rebecca** and I go to preschool,

My best friend is **Poppy**, who is really cool.

I watch **Peppa Pig** on TV,

Playing **in muddy puddles** is lots of fun for me.

I just love **mashed potato** to eat,

And sometimes **Janet's cheese straws** for a treat.

Purple is a colour I like a lot,

My **electric Audi car** is the best present I ever got.

My favourite person is **my brother, Nathan**, who is

a gem,

So this, my first poem, is just for them!

Rebecca Lanham (2)

Seashells Nursery, Mablethorpe

160

My First Poem

My name is Owen and I go to preschool,

My best friend is Blue, who is really cool.

I watch PAW Patrol, Fireman Sam and Blaze on TV,

Playing outside is lots of fun for me.

I just love sausages to eat,

And sometimes chocolate for a treat.

Orange is a colour I like a lot,

My cement mixer is the best present I ever got.

My favourite person is Janet, who is a gem,

So this, my first poem, is just for them!

Owen Hallam (2)

Seashells Nursery, Mablethorpe

My First Poem

My name is **Darcie-Leigh** and I go to preschool,

My best friend is **Ethan**, who is really cool.

I watch **Frozen and CBeebies** on TV,

Playing **with my toys and friends** is lots of fun

for me.

I just love **any food** to eat,

And sometimes **chocolate and sweets** for a treat.

Pink is a colour I like a lot,

My **Peppa Pig stuff** are the best presents I ever got.

My favourite people are **Mummy and Daddy**, who

are gems,

So this, my first poem, is just for them!

Darcie-Leigh Chapman (2)

Seashells Nursery, Mablethorpe

162

My First Poem

My name is **Alfie** and I go to preschool,
My best friend is **Rohan**, who is really cool.
I watch **Postman Pat** on TV,
Playing **doctors** is lots of fun for me.
I just love **pasta** to eat,
And sometimes **sweets** for a treat.
Orange is a colour I like a lot,
My **Fireman Sam engine** is the best present I
ever got.
My favourite person is **Nannie**, who is a gem,
So this, my first poem, is just for them!

Alfie Roach-Cowan (3)

Serendipitys Day Nursery, Newark

My First Poem

My name is Tom and I go to preschool,

My best friends are Kai and Zac, who are really cool.

I watch Go Jetters on TV,

Playing with my Lego is lots of fun for me.

I just love bananas to eat,

And sometimes Mummy's flapjack for a treat.

Red is a colour I like a lot,

My bike is the best present I ever got.

My favourite people are Mummy and Daddy, who are gems,

So this, my first poem, is just for them!

Tom Clarke (3)

Serendipitys Day Nursery, Newark

My First Poem

My name is Genevieve and I go to preschool,
My best friend is Finley, who is really cool.
I watch Labyrinth and Snow White on TV,
Playing Duck, Duck, Goose is lots of fun for me.
I just love slurpy spaghetti to eat,
And sometimes cake for a treat.
Purple is a colour I like a lot,
My bee is the best present I ever got.
My favourite person is straight hair Olivia, who is
a gem,
So this, my first poem, is just for them!

Genevieve Blunt (4)

Serendipitys Day Nursery, Newark

165

My First Poem

My name is **Zach** and I go to preschool,

My best friend is **Theo**, who is really cool.

I watch **Postman Pat** on TV,

Playing **egg hunting** is lots of fun for me.

I just love **cheese** to eat,

And sometimes **ice cream** for a treat.

Green is a colour I like a lot,

My **CD player** is the best present I ever got.

My favourite person is **Daddy**, who is a gem,

So this, my first poem, is just for them!

Zach Charlesworth (3)

Serendipitys Day Nursery, Newark

My First Poem

My name is Daniel and I go to preschool,
My best friend is Maddy, who is really cool.
I watch Stick Man on TV,
Playing with building blocks is lots of fun for me.
I just love vegetable soup to eat,
And sometimes chocolate cake for a treat.
Light blue is a colour I like a lot,
My Skye toy from PAW Patrol is the best present
I ever got.
My favourite person is Mummy, who is a gem,
So this, my first poem, is just for them!

Daniel John Franks (4)

Serendipitys Day Nursery, Newark

My First Poem

My name is **Caleb** and I go to preschool,

My best friend is **Mac**, who is really cool.

I watch **Thunderbirds** on TV,

Playing **outside** is lots of fun for me.

I just love **chocolate** to eat,

And sometimes **ice lollies** for a treat.

Red is a colour I like a lot,

My **pirate ship** is the best present I ever got.

My favourite person is **Molly**, who is a gem,

So this, my first poem, is just for them!

Caleb West (4)

Serendipitys Day Nursery, Newark

My First Poem

My name is **Macy-Rose** and I go to preschool,

My best friend is **Megan**, who is really cool.

I watch **Peppa Pig and Bing** on TV,

Playing **football** is lots of fun for me.

I just love **fish, fruit, and cheese and ham toasties** to eat,

And sometimes **ice cream** for a treat.

Red is a colour I like a lot,

My **farmyard/zoo** is the best present I ever got.

My favourite person is **Alastair**, who is a gem,

So this, my first poem, is just for them!

Macy-Rose Sheppard-Cooper (3)

Shardlow Hall Private Day Nursery, Derby

My First Poem

My name is Noah and I go to preschool,

My best friend is Ethan, who is really cool.

I watch Peppa Pig and snooker on TV,

Playing dinosaurs is lots of fun for me.

I just love chocolate pops to eat,

And sometimes ice cream for a treat.

Red is a colour I like a lot,

My snooker table is the best present I ever got.

My favourite person is Uncle Bobby, who is a gem,

So this, my first poem, is just for them!

Noah Hutchinson-Backer (3)

Shardlow Hall Private Day Nursery, Derby

My First Poem

My name is Logan and I go to preschool,
My best friend is William, who is really cool.
I watch Ninja Warrior on TV,
Playing with toy cars is lots of fun for me.
I just love carrots to eat,
And sometimes Jumping Jelly Babies for a treat.
Blue is a colour I like a lot,
My Gooey Louie is the best present I ever got.
My favourite person is Grandad, who is a gem,
So this, my first poem, is just for them!

Logan Worthington (4)
Shardlow Hall Private Day Nursery, Derby

My First Poem

My name is Henry and I go to preschool,

My best friend is Moses, who is really cool.

I watch Peppa Pig on TV,

Playing dressing up is lots of fun for me.

I just love sandwiches to eat,

And sometimes chocolate for a treat.

Brown is a colour I like a lot,

My Spider-Man is the best present I ever got.

My favourite person is Dylan, who is a gem,

So this, my first poem, is just for them!

Henry Quilter (4)

Sinfin Community Childcare, Derby

My First Poem

My name is Sophia and I go to preschool,
My best friend is Lola, who is really cool.
I watch Scooby-Doo on TV,
Playing with cars is lots of fun for me.
I just love chips and sauce to eat,
And sometimes sweeties for a treat.
Blue is a colour I like a lot,
My Spider-Man is the best present I ever got.
My favourite person is Charley, who is a gem,
So this, my first poem, is just for them!

Sophia Platt (4)
Sinfin Community Childcare, Derby

My First Poem

My name is **Sebastian** and I go to preschool,

My best friend is **Dylan**, who is really cool.

I watch **Teenage Mutant Ninja Turtles** on TV,

Playing **with building blocks** is lots of fun for me.

I just love **fish fingers** to eat,

And sometimes **chocolate** for a treat.

Blue is a colour I like a lot,

My **Spider-Man costume** is the best present I

ever got.

My favourite person is **Daddy**, who is a gem,

So this, my first poem, is just for them!

Sebastian Bainbridge (3)

Sinfin Community Childcare, Derby

My First Poem

My name is Isaac and I go to preschool,
My best friend is Lola, who is really cool.
I watch Peppa Pig on TV,
Playing with cars is lots of fun for me.
I just love chicken nuggets to eat,
And sometimes biscuits for a treat.
Red is a colour I like a lot,
My Minion toys are the best presents I ever got.
My favourite person is Mummy, who is a gem,
So this, my first poem, is just for them!

Isaac Paul Holland (3)

Sinfin Community Childcare, Derby

175

My First Poem

My name is **Lola** and I go to preschool,

My best friend is **Isaac**, who is really cool.

I watch **dancing shows** on TV,

Playing **Little People** is lots of fun for me.

I just love **carrots** to eat,

And sometimes **pizza** for a treat.

Purple is a colour I like a lot,

My **Lucy doll and Baby Annabell** are the best

presents I ever got.

My favourite person is **Jess**, who is a gem,

So this, my first poem, is just for them!

Lola Amanda Radford (3)

Sinfin Community Childcare, Derby

My First Poem

My name is Alex and I go to preschool,

My best friend is Jools, who is really cool.

I watch monsters on TV,

Playing running, jumping and skipping is lots of
fun for me.

I just love apple to eat,

And sometimes Smarties for a treat.

Blue is a colour I like a lot,

My racing car is the best present I ever got.

My favourite person is Jools, who is a gem,

So this, my first poem, is just for them!

Alex Rowland (4)

St Michael's Preschool, Peterborough

My First Poem

My name is Harry and I go to preschool,

My best friends are Harvey, Bea and Lottie, who
are really cool.

I watch CBeebies on TV,

Playing with washing machines and Hoovers is
lots of fun for me.

I just love chips to eat,

And sometimes a Kinder bar for a treat.

Blue is a colour I like a lot,

My washing machine is the best present I ever got.

My favourite person is Nona, who is a gem,

So this, my first poem, is just for them!

Harry Crofts (3)

St Michael's Preschool, Peterborough

My First Poem

My name is Sasha and I go to preschool,
My best friend is Mummy, who is really cool.
I watch Peppa Pig on TV,
Playing with Pinypon is lots of fun for me.
I just love mashed potato to eat,
And sometimes sweeties and chocolate for
a treat.
Blue is a colour I like a lot,
My Pinypon hotel and campervan are the best
presents I ever got.
My favourite person is Mummy, who is a gem,
So this, my first poem, is just for them!

Sasha Weir (3)
St Michael's Preschool, Peterborough

My First Poem

My name is **Harvey** and I go to preschool,

My best friend is **Alfie**, who is really cool.

I watch **Scooby-Doo** on TV,

Playing **with Lego and cars** is lots of fun for me.

I just love **cheese spread** to eat,

And sometimes **sweets** for a treat.

Green is a colour I like a lot,

My **guitar** is the best present I ever got.

My favourite person is **George**, who is a gem,

So this, my first poem, is just for them!

Harvey Wise (3)

St Michael's Preschool, Peterborough

My First Poem

My name is Amelia and I go to preschool,
My best friend is Mummy, who is really cool.
I watch Topsy and Tim on TV,
Playing with toys is lots of fun for me.
I just love pizza to eat,
And sometimes chocolate for a treat.
Pink is a colour I like a lot,
My Frozen toys are the best presents I ever got.
My favourite person is Euza, who is a gem,
So this, my first poem, is just for them!

Amelia Sharin (4)
Stepping Stones Preschool, Smethwick

My First Poem

My name is **Ewan** and I go to preschool,

My best friend is **Saffron**, who is really cool.

I watch **Fireman Sam** on TV,

Playing **with Lego** is lots of fun for me.

I just love **jacket potato** to eat,

And sometimes **sweets** for a treat.

Red is a colour I like a lot,

My **cow farm** is the best present I ever got.

My favourite person is **Mommy**, who is a gem,

So this, my first poem, is just for them!

Ewan Roy Tyler-Stevens (3)

Stepping Stones Preschool, Smethwick

My First Poem

My name is Evie and I go to preschool,
My best friend is Daddy, who is really cool.
I watch Peppa Pig on TV,
Playing with dollies is lots of fun for me.
I just love pasta to eat,
And sometimes biscuits for a treat.
Purple is a colour I like a lot,
My Elsa doll is the best present I ever got.
My favourite person is Daddy, who is a gem,
So this, my first poem, is just for them!

Evie Rose Beale (3)
Stepping Stones Preschool, Smethwick

My First Poem

My name is **Preet** and I go to preschool,

My best friend is **Simran**, who is really cool.

I watch **Peppa Pig** on TV,

Playing **with toys** is lots of fun for me.

I just love **sweets** to eat,

And sometimes **ice cream** for a treat.

Pink is a colour I like a lot,

My **Peppa Pig birthday cake** is the best present I ever got.

My favourite person is **Daddy**, who is a gem,

So this, my first poem, is just for them!

Preet Chahal (2)
Stepping Stones Preschool, Smethwick

My First Poem

My name is Amina and I go to preschool,
My best friend is Umar, who is really cool.
I watch Mr Tumble on TV,
Playing with toys is lots of fun for me.
I just love chapatis to eat,
And sometimes sweets for a treat.
Pink is a colour I like a lot,
My make-up is the best present I ever got.
My favourite person is Daddy, who is a gem,
So this, my first poem, is just for them!

Amina Nisa (4)

Stepping Stones Preschool, Smethwick

My First Poem

My name is Shian and I go to preschool,

My best friend is Nadia, who is really cool.

I watch Peppa Pig on TV,

Playing with toys is lots of fun for me.

I just love breakfast to eat,

And sometimes sweets for a treat.

Blue is a colour I like a lot,

My sunglasses are the best present I ever got.

My favourite person is Daddy, who is a gem,

So this, my first poem, is just for them!

Shian Pirout (3)
Stepping Stones Preschool, Smethwick

My First Poem

My name is Isha and I go to preschool,
My best friend is Sofia, who is really cool.
I watch Dora the Explorer on TV,
Playing tiger is lots of fun for me.
I just love sandwiches to eat,
And sometimes grapes for a treat.
Pink is a colour I like a lot,
My mermaid doll is the best present I ever got.
My favourite person is Grandma, who is a gem,
So this, my first poem, is just for them!

Isha Kaur (3)
Stepping Stones Preschool, Smethwick

My First Poem

My name is **Gursimran** and I go to preschool,

My best friend is **Abbey**, who is really cool.

I watch **Mr Bean** on TV,

Playing **with toys** is lots of fun for me.

I just love **beans on toast** to eat,

And sometimes **pink sweets** for a treat.

Pink is a colour I like a lot,

My **princess** is the best present I ever got.

My favourite person is **Daddy**, who is a gem,

So this, my first poem, is just for them!

Gursimran Kaur (4)

Stepping Stones Preschool, Smethwick

My First Poem

My name is Caleb and I go to preschool,

My best friend is Phoebe, who is really cool.

I watch Power Rangers Dino Charge on TV,

Playing with toy cars is lots of fun for me.

I just love chocolate spread sandwiches to eat,

And sometimes sweeties for a treat.

Black is a colour I like a lot,

My Batman Lego is the best present I ever got.

My favourite person is my brother Ryan, who is

a gem,

So this, my first poem, is just for them!

Caleb Silver (4)

Sunny Days Preschool, High Wycombe

My First Poem

My name is Sabrina and I go to preschool,

My best friend is Neveah, who is really cool.

I watch Ben & Holly on TV,

Playing with the iPad is lots of fun for me.

I just love boiled eggs to eat,

And sometimes chocolate cake for a treat.

Pink is a colour I like a lot,

My Anna doll is the best present I ever got.

My favourite person is Mummy, who is a gem,

So this, my first poem, is just for them!

Sabrina Amara Hussain (4)

Teddies Day Nursery, Oldham

My First Poem

My name is Jaymee and I go to preschool,

My best friend is Ella, who is really cool.

I watch Lion King on TV,

Playing jigsaws is lots of fun for me.

I just love jelly to eat,

And sometimes cakes for a treat.

Black is a colour I like a lot,

My Elsa doll is the best present I ever got.

My favourite person is Leo, who is a gem,

So this, my first poem, is just for them!

Jaymee Ann Corbishley (4)

Teddies Day Nursery, Oldham

My First Poem

My name is Chiasa and I go to preschool,

My best friend is Hunter, who is really cool.

I watch Mr Bean on TV,

Playing with Play-Doh is lots of fun for me.

I just love bananas to eat,

And sometimes chocolate for a treat.

Black is a colour I like a lot,

My Kindle is the best present I ever got.

My favourite person is Mummy, who is a gem,

So this, my first poem, is just for them!

Chiasa Etugo (4)

Teddies Day Nursery, Oldham

My First Poem

My name is Holly and I go to preschool,

My best friend is Orla, who is really cool.

I watch Adia on TV,

Playing Where is Mummy? is lots of fun for me.

I just love sweets to eat,

And sometimes cake for a treat.

Yellow, orange and red are colours I like a lot,

My sweets and cake are the best presents I ever got.

My favourite person is my sister, who is a gem,

So this, my first poem, is just for them!

Holly Mari-Beth Walsh (4)

Teddies Day Nursery, Oldham

My First Poem

My name is **Brayden** and I go to preschool,

My best friend is **Jaime**, who is really cool.

I watch **Masha and the Bear** on TV,

Playing **Duplo** is lots of fun for me.

I just love **tuna fish sandwiches** to eat,

And sometimes **a picnic** for a treat.

Blue and orange are colours I like a lot,

My **big Thomas** is the best present I ever got.

My favourite people are **Mummy and Daddy**, who

are gems,

So this, my first poem, is just for them!

Brayden Ashworth (3)

Teddies Day Nursery, Oldham

My First Poem

My name is **Nevaeh** and I go to preschool,

My best friend is **Nevaeh B**, who is really cool.

I watch **CBeebies and Nick Junior** on TV,

Playing **with paints** is lots of fun for me.

I just love **lasagne** to eat,

And sometimes **chocolate** for a treat.

Pink is a colour I like a lot,

My **Hello Kitty bracelet kit** is the best present I

ever got.

My favourite person is **my baby brother, Shae**, who

is a gem,

So this, my first poem, is just for them!

Nevaeh Caines-Rahman (4)

Teddies Day Nursery, Oldham

My First Poem

My name is George and I go to preschool,

My best friend is Tyler, who is really cool.

I watch Max Steel, Scooby-Doo
and Transformers on TV,

Playing Duplo is lots of fun for me.

I just love fish fingers, waffles and cheese and
onion pie to eat,

And sometimes cake for a treat.

Red is a colour I like a lot,

My Hulk Buster is the best present I ever got.

My favourite person is Mummy, who is a gem,

So this, my first poem, is just for them!

George Roy Grady (4)

Teddies Day Nursery, Oldham

My First Poem

My name is Orla and I go to preschool,
My best friends are Jaymee, Naveah
and Brayden, who are really cool.
I watch Peppa Pig and Team Umizoomi on TV,
Playing with Olaf, Anna, Elsa and my
doll's house is lots of fun for me.
I just love Coco Pops, Weetabix
and Cornflakes to eat,
And sometimes chocolate eggs for a treat.
Pink is a colour I like a lot,
My doll's house is the best present I ever got.
My favourite people are Mummy, Daddy and
Kieran, who are gems,
So this, my first poem, is just for them!

Orla Mary Corbishley (4)
Teddies Day Nursery, Oldham

My First Poem

We hope you have enjoyed reading this book – and that you will continue to enjoy it in the coming years.

If you're a young writer who enjoys reading and creative writing, or the parent of an enthusiastic poet or story writer, do visit our websites, www.myfirstpoem.com and www.youngwriters.co.uk. Here you will find free competitions, workshops and games, as well as recommended reads, a poetry glossary and our blog.

If you would like to order further copies of this book, or any of our other titles, then please give us a call or visit www.myfirstpoem.com.

My First Poem
Remus House
Coltsfoot Drive
Peterborough
PE2 9BF

Tel: 01733 898110
info@myfirstpoem.com